Character Education

Honesty

by Lucia Raatma

Consultant:
Thomas Lickona, Ph.D.
Center for the 4th and 5th Rs
New York State University at Cortland

Bridgestone Books
an imprint of Capstone Press
Mankato, Minnesota

Bridgestone Books are published by Capstone Press
818 North Willow Street, Mankato, Minnesota 56001
http://www.capstone-press.com

Library of Congress Cataloging-in-Publication Data
Raatma, Lucia.
    Honesty/by Lucia Raatma.
        p. cm.—(Character education)
    Includes bibliographical references and index.
    Summary: Explains the virtue of honesty and how readers can practice it at
home, in the community, and with each other.
    ISBN 0-7368-0369-6
    1. Honesty—Juvenile literature. [1. Honesty.] I. Title. II. Series.
BJ1533.H7R23   2000
179'.9—dc21
                                                                99-23766
                                                                    CIP

Editorial Credits

Christy Steele, editor; Heather Kindseth, cover designer and illustrator;
    Kimberly Danger, photo researcher

Photo Credits

International Stock/Joe Willis, cover
Photo Network/Esbin-Anderson, 4, 6; Myrleen Ferguson, 10
Shaffer Photography/James L. Shaffer, 8, 12
Visuals Unlimited, 20; Visuals Unlimited/Mark E. Gibson, 14; Bernd
    Wittich, 16; Jeff Greenberg, 18

Table of Contents

Honesty

Honesty means being truthful. Honest people do what is right. Honest people do not lie or cheat. Be honest with yourself, your parents, and your friends. People will trust you if you are honest.

cheat
to trick others to get what you want

Being Honest with Yourself

Everyone has problems. You should admit your problems to yourself. But you do not have to solve your problems on your own. Do not be afraid to talk about them. Other people can help you if you are honest about your problems.

admit
to agree that something is true

Honesty with Your Parents

Your parents can help you if you are honest with them. You can tell your parents how you feel. Tell them when you are upset or afraid. Tell your parents when you make a mistake. Being honest allows your parents to trust you and to help you.

Honesty with Your Friends

Good friends are honest. Honest friends do not tell lies or break their promises. You should do what you tell your friends you will do. Honest people keep friends' secrets. Honest people do not take things without asking.

Honesty in Games

Honest people are fair when they play games. Every game has rules you should follow. Honest people do not break the rules in order to win. Friends will play with you if you are honest and follow the rules.

Honesty at School

Honest people follow rules at school. They do not cheat on tests. Honest people do not copy someone else's work. You will feel good when you have earned your own grade.

Honesty in Your Community

Honesty makes a community a good place to live. Be honest with your neighbors. Tell them if you break their windows while playing baseball. Sometimes store clerks give people too much change. Honest people return this extra money.

Honest Abe

Abraham Lincoln was so truthful that people called him Honest Abe. He was a lawyer. Abraham did not lie to win cases. People trusted him because he was honest. Abraham's honesty helped him become president of the United States.

lawyer

a person who helps people understand the law; lawyers act and speak for people in court.

Honesty and You

Honesty is important in your life. People will trust and respect you if you are honest. Being honest will help you make and keep friends. You will feel good about yourself if you are honest.

Hands On: Make a Lost-and-Found Box

Keeping things that are not yours is not honest. You can make a lost-and-found box to return things you find.

What You Need

A large cardboard box
Markers

What You Do

1. Write the words "Lost and Found" on the outside of the box.
2. Use the markers to decorate the box.
3. Ask your teacher if you can place the box in the back of your classroom.
4. Tell students to place any items they find in the box.

People can look in the box for things they have lost.
Honest people will take only the items that belong to them.

Words to Know

admit (ad-MIT)—to agree that something is true

cheat (CHEET)—to trick someone to get what you want

lawyer (LAW-yur)—a person who is trained to advise people about the law; lawyers act and speak for people in court.

mistake (muh-STAKE)—something that you do wrong

promise (PROM-iss)—to give your word that you will do something

Read More

Adams, Lisa K. *Dealing with Lying.* The Conflict Resolution Library. New York: PowerKids Press, 1997.
Mosher, Kiki. *Learning about Honesty from the Life of Abraham Lincoln.* A Character Building Book. New York: PowerKids Press, 1996.
Snyder, Margaret. *Honesty.* Doing the Right Thing. Vero Beach, Fla.: Rourke, 1999.

Internet Sites

Adventures from the Book of Virtues Home Page
http://www.pbs.org/adventures
Character Counts! National Homepage
http://www.charactercounts.org/index.htm
The History Place Presents Abraham Lincoln
http://www.historyplace.com/lincoln

Index